The Onion, Memory

The
Onion,
Memory

Craig Raine

Oxford   New York
OXFORD UNIVERSITY PRESS

Oxford University Press, Walton Street, Oxford OX2 6DP
Oxford New York Toronto
Delhi Bombay Calcutta Madras Karachi
Petaling Jaya Singapore Hong Kong Tokyo
Nairobi Dar es Salaam Cape Town
Melbourne Auckland
and associated companies in
Berlin Ibadan

Oxford is a trade mark of Oxford University Press

© Oxford University Press 1978

First published 1978
Reprinted 1980, 1981, 1983, 1986, 1990

British Library Cataloguing in Publication Data
Raine, Craig
The onion, memory.
I. Title
821'.9'14   PR6068.A/   77–30527
ISBN 0–19–211877–3

Printed in Hong Kong

Contents

Acknowledgements

Some of these poems first appeared in the *New Statesman*, the *New Review*, the *London Magazine*, *The Honest Ulsterman*, the *Observer*, *The Times Literary Supplement*, *P.E.N. New Poems 1977*, Faber & Faber's *Poetry Introduction 4*, *Green Lines*, *Vogue*. 'Anno Domini' was printed by the *New Review*.

YELLOW PAGES

The Butcher

'And even St George—if Gibbon is correct—wore a top hat once;
ıe was an army contractor and supplied indifferent bacon'
                                    —E M Forster : *Abinger Harvest*

Surrounded by sausages, the butcher stands
smoking a pencil like Isambard Kingdom Brunel . . .

He duels with himself and woos his women customers,
offering thin coiled coral necklaces of mince,

heart lamé-ed from the fridge, a leg of pork
like a nasty bouquet, pound notes printed with blood.

He knows all about nudity—the slap and trickle
of blood, chickens stripped to their aertex vests.

He rips the gauze from dead balletic pigs,
and makes the bacon slicer swish its legs.

How the customers laugh ! His striped apron
gets as dirty as the mattress in a brothel . . .

At 10, he drinks his tea with the spoon held back,
and the *Great Eastern* goes straight to the bottom.

The Barber

The barber bows with kazoo breath
and antlered chromium clippers to plough a neck.

Or flies electric shears fringed with steel
from a row where they sleep like bats.

His scissors scandal-monger round the ears,
cut fringes with a sudden coaldust on the face.

A chain of greasy hair is woven in his comb.
He rubs a gout of Brylcreem with pipe-smoking palms,

massages the scalp like a concert pianist,
then paints the iron-filings off a face.

He washes his wrists like a fly,
takes pay, and waits for another piece

of sheeted furniture to sit there and be dusted . . .
He dreams of making hay, while the wireless shines.

The Gardener

Up and down the lawn he walks with cycling hands
that tremble on the mower's stethoscope.

Creases blink behind his knees.
He stares at a prance of spray

and wrestles with Leviathan alone. Victorious,
he bangs the grass box empty like a clog . . .

The shears are a Y that wants to be an X—
he holds them like a water diviner,

and hangs them upside down, a wish-bone.
His hands row gently on the plunger

and detonate the earth. He smacks the clods
and dandles weeds on trembling prongs.

They lie, a heap of dusters softly shaken out.
At night he plays a pattering hose, fanned

like a drummer's brush. His aim is to grow
the Kremlin—the roses' tight pink cupolas

ring bells . . . For this he stands in weariness,
tired as a teapot, feeling the small of his back.

4

The Grocer

'the kingdom of God cometh not with observation'
— James Joyce to Lady Gregory

The grocer's hair is parted like a feather
by two swift brushes and a dab of brilliantine.

His cheesewire is a sun-dial selling by the hour.
He brings it down at four and five o'clock,

the wooden T gripped like a corkscrew.
Greaseproof squares curl in diamonds on a hook.

He takes, and orientates the chock of cheese,
swoops his hand away, leaves it on the choppy scales.

Tortoise-necked, he reads the price aloud
and fingers do their automatic origami.

He shakes the air into a paper bag and,
eggs pickpocketed inside, trapezes it.

Coins are raked with trident hand,
trickled into the till—palm out,

with thumb crooked over the stigma,
he smiles like a modest quattrocento Christ.

5

The Ice Cream Man

'So again Kingfishers, when they catch a fish, always beat it until it is killed; and in the Zoological Gardens they always beat the raw meat, with which they are sometimes fed, before devouring it' —Charles Darwin : *The Expression of the Emotions in Man & Animals*

A silver comma clenched between his teeth,
he filled the pause of childhood with adventure—

reaching for his wonky telescope of cornets
or his Mabbot's of Manchester wafer-machine.

We watched him greedily as Darwin at the zoo
after the scream of his tropical beak :

he worked with hairy deaf and dumb hands,
agile as a pair of courting spiders,

with monkeys' blood in a circumcised bottle.
We pressed his sandwiches till they oozed like brie

and nibbled cornets down to thimbles—
bit by bit, the way I must invent him now . . .

Charlie Carlo, dead skull,
faceless as the pom-poms from his scoop.

He converted us. We came as savages
and left like a procession at Lourdes.

The Tattooed Man

Someone, God perhaps, has scribbled
hair all over his chest and shoulders—

but the drawings are there underneath.
He sits on a bench in his braces,

advertising anchors and bluebirds
and the bruised names of love . . .

He is a suitcase with exotic labels,
his precious common things inside.

Girls have held him fiercely, as if
he was everything they owned.

He looks like lost property now.
I read his crowded arms

and think of tattooed gravestones—
love letters lost in all the long grass.

The Window Cleaner

The college quad is cobbled like a blackberry
and shining in the rain and dangerous . . .

The window cleaner cups a telescopic caber—
Blondin never trod so warily.

He wears a sad expression on his face,
half a dress, and heather-mixture trews—

all day he listens to the squeak of puppies,
litters he is paid to drown and strangle.

All day he sees himself in the glass darkly
and waves goodbye, goodbye, goodbye.

All day he wrings his hands, crying buckets.
He'd rather shave shop windows clean

than climb this bendy Jacob's ladder
and risk the washboard fall of seraphim . . .

THE SIGNIFICANCE OF NOTHING

An Enquiry into Two Inches of Ivory

We live in the great indoors :
the vacuum cleaner grazes
over the carpet, lowing,
its udder a swollen wobble . . .

At night, the switches stare
from every wall like flat-faced
barn-owls, and light ripens
the electric pear.

Esse is percipi—Berkeley knew
the gentle irony of objects, how
they told amusing lies and drew laughter,
if only we believed our eyes.

Daily things. Objects
in the museum of ordinary art.
Two armless Lilliputian queens
preside, watching a giant bathe.
He catches the slippery cubist fish
with perfumed eggs. Another
is a yogi on the scrubbing brush.
Water painlessly breaks his bent
Picasso legs.

Clothes queue up in the wardrobe,
an echo to the eye, or a jangle of Euclid.
The wall-phone wears a pince-nez
even in the dark—the flex
is Jewish orthodox.

Day begins.
The milkman delivers
penguins with their chinking atonal fuss.
Cups commemorate the War
of Jenkins' Ear.
Without thinking, the giant
puts a kettle on the octopus.

Demolition with Tobacco Speck

'The man in the brown macintosh loves a lady who is dead'
— James Joyce : *Ulysses*

Hic, haec, hoc—the dead language
of bricks tipping from a barrow.

Air is permed above an open petrol can.
Two bulldozers move on crêpe soles.
The JCB grasps things at the wrong
angle, like a baby, and hesitates
before it half drops, half
puts them down.

Like Rembrandt's *Brace and Bit*
with Holy Family and Angels, wistful
details touch the hem of all experience.

A fire flexes its flayed musculature,
crazy with neglect . . .

The mind imagines how the house will fall—
The whole façade a fainting drawbridge,
followed by a broken octave
slowing to the waggle of
a penny dropped.

Straight down,
four storeys drop as one.
It is the brief unveiling of a dusty
statue, swaying on a plinth of rubble . . .

Delicately, the foreman's tongue
feels along his bottom lip,
finding a tobacco speck.

Houses in North Oxford

are on parade, inspected by the sun
who looks them in the eyes and strikes
his medals on the spot . . .

Row on row of red-brick guards,
with window boxes boasting battle ribbons
from the Spring campaign. They stand

at attention : the cars a line of
impeccable boots, all at an angle
of one hundred and eighty degrees;

bay windows bulging like holsters;
rifles clamped to their sides.
Not one soldier moves, unless

you happen to see the slow
confident wink of a blind being drawn . . .
The gardens lay out kit—

spick privet, polished laurels,
the larch's tiny hand grenades,
pipe-clayed lilies of the valley—

while Keble sprawls at ease, handsome
in mufti, the general in Fair-Isles,
his Sam Browne dangling like a fire-escape.

Who would guess from this the timid heart—
the wounded professor, nuns on their knees,
the dear old thing afraid of a khaki envelope?

14

Misericords

It is a world without heroes,
without abstractions, without combs—
everyone has hair like bark . . .

Shiny as a coalman's sack,
they are postcards from the continent
of darkest dailiness, diaries
by the English negro.

Multitudes shrink to a pigmy pair
in an Eden without eyelashes :
the woman rises from the waves
of wood, a Venus Anadyomene,
pride in the piled
plumpness of belly—yeasty,
deep-navelled, a risen cottage loaf.
Her nose peels in August like a Jersey potato.

The man is dull silver
like burnished dirt
on the heel of a hand.

About to kiss, they slope together,
crooked gothic type, with whistling mouths
pushed out like daffodils.
Envy sneers with trumpeter's lips.

They are as ordinary as water,
these epiphanies under the seat—
humble backs, bumpy as laburnum pods,
that plough the grain,
a merry-go-round of gulls
behind the tilted share.

Tooth-ache, tragedy and top notes
share a mask of facial palsy
in this alliterative world.
Beside a pool,
boys prepare to dive
with hands in prayer . . .

In the end, the detail reaches out :
nature's ivory mandolin
with inlaid ebony seeds,
the outside speckled
like a thrush's egg—
half a pear with a broken
stalk . . .

Sitting on a kitchen chair
by the great cathedral door,
the custodian knits.

With wheedling beaks,
her brilliant needles bill and coo.

Bed & Breakfast

The peach is thick with dust :
it has lain all night like Pharaoh
in the attic of the dark.

Halved and tilted,
the pock-marked stone removed,
juices run into the roof of its mouth.

The tea cools to a dead silver—
a skin that gathers and heals
like something alive.

Bread develops slowly under the grill,
a Polaroid picture of desert :
above it, the air is almost in tears

The gas plops out,
and I butter the toast
listening to matches struck in the dark.

As I enter with the lacquered tray,
you draw back the curtain like time :
five pink farrow suckle at each foot.

The ticking on the mattress is ploughed in strips.
Tea and toast with cunty fingers.
Bed and breakfast.

The Book of the Market

begins and ends *in medias res*,
a classically 'indifferent whole'.
We wander through it like Casaubon, clutching
lists we've pencilled on the backs of envelopes.

Tomatoes kiss
with puckered lips, drooling
ichor from their broken skins.
Their colour clamours to be fed :
we prod them gently, bring our faces
close like mothers bending over babies,
as if to shush that red.
The prawns respond by crooking
helpless fingers, tiny segments
soft as sucking blisters.
The raspberries are nursing nipples . . .

We potter calmly like Casaubon,
clutching the key to all mythologies,
a shopping list. Among the butcher's
bric-a-brac, a cameo
cut on a conch of Wiltshire ham—
five milky roads divide some reddish fields
ploughed neatly as a fingerprint, calm
as a corpse.

Everywhere, *memento mori*—
the turnip's scar is written here;
onions trundle from a pelican scoop
like anarchist bombs; the cobs of corn
are similes for nooses neatly tied;
lobsters and crabs, breastplates and pliers,

18

wirecutters and greaves, blending the vocabulary
of different wars . . .

Strawberries resume a sub-plot
of revolt, a peasant rising :
the ringleaders' heads arranged in punnets,
sunburnt, pitted, unshaven.
Grapes are held aloft, their shining sacs
jostle like traitorous bowels . . .

There is no end, except that,
in medias res, the kippers'
quotidian violins assume the antique tones
and smokey varnish of Cremona.
We see the carrots under glass,
as items in a treasure house—
each bunch an old Elizabethan gauntlet,
the tapered fingers creased with wear . . .

The Fair in St Giles

The showman's coat is frogged and braided
like a saxophone, his barker pregnant

with the drum : they are odder, really,
than their *Famous Collection of Cobras*

who rear like second-hand ladles . . .
At the shooting range, customers break

the rifles in two, nuzzle the stocks
like hungry cats and fire (miaow !)

at clay-pipe periscopes. The tin
is pock-marked as a Pakistani's cheek.

I tear at my mohair candy floss and watch
a winner shake the vaccinated coconuts :

a wary man tees up the rest, sneaking
behind the tarpaulin like Polonius.

The Dodgems bully-off and then subside
to the shambles of a cobbler's shop;

scissor-legged in jodhpurs,
riders smoke outside the Wall of Death;

the stripper crooks her knees in turn,
a bird's nest underneath each arm—

all things vivid as a dreamed adultery . . .
A man in black soliloquizes,

denounces all our disappointment,
his nose a terrible thimble.

In the Woods

Always at this time there is the bankrupt plant :
autumn afflicts the failed machinery of ferns with rust.
The foliage is full of broken windows.
The birch trees shed their aluminium crust,

and the cedar drops its complicated cogs.
The roof of things has fallen in—
these paprika patches on the factory floor
are corrugated remnants of protective tin.

Oddments blacken strangely on a nearby fence :
rags, an old glove in a liquorice droop,
washleathers warp with dull black holly claws.
It is a sad, abandoned, oddly human group.

The glove is singular. You cannot try it on.
It is too small. Besides, it has no fingers.
It is more like something surgical—
the unpleasant shape of stumpy enigmas.

Below, a nylon sock curls up like a dead animal.
Through a hole in the toe, a glint of teeth.
Over there, the remains of a fire—
pigeon feathers in a narrow ashy wreath.

And everywhere egg-shells, egg-shells,
so light they stir with the gentlest breath—
a breakfast of papery skulls. The Omelette Man
has eaten here and manufactured death.

Meditation at Spring Hill

No, this afternoon I do not think so.
A god might once have seen
in this white stone house
somewhere to go,
a dry oasis of white solitude,
a scrap of desert unsubdued
by the constant sluice
of green, of green, of green.
But I do not think so this afternoon.

Here the cows cough
or harmonize a croon
and sway in single file,
syncopated, high-assed, Harlem style,
towards a slateblue water trough
to quench their thirst.
No, here one comes to know
the lonely God who made the cow
to fill his empty Eden first,
and afterwards made man.
Their eyes, opaquely sad,
recall some negro pianist
muddy with dope and blues—
first try of some perfectionist
gone out of use.

One might learn to be glad
of cows if one began
living here. This white stone house has stood
since Shakespeare in its sage green ocean,
but when a saw wheezes through a piece of wood
at night, laughing, short of wind,

its stone might be an abstract notion
in some vegetable mind . . .

Through fog as thick as phlegm
the cows advance reproachfully,
as if we were the gods who made and left them.
We watch them chew and spill
a bitter spew of chlorophyl.

Memory

It is being blind in sunlight,
with one shy hand on Cotswold stone,
waiting for names to speak themselves.

It is the sense of emptiness,
the unshaven feel of Cotswold stone,
and then the fingers saying father . . .

Or else breath stumbles, and
a river is the grey silk dress,
because a mallard pulls a puckering strand.

It is the morning office block,
dimly lit with tacking stitches, yet
finished as regret. Faint threads

that blaze at evening . . .
It is the staircase we can never climb,
the ruined spiral of the silver birch,

dripping cobwebs . . .
It is the child who remembers nothing,
and weeps with holly-pointed lashes.

ALL THE INVENTORY OF FLESH

The Onion, Memory

Divorced, but friends again at last,
we walk old ground together
in bright blue uncomplicated weather.
We laugh and pause
to hack to bits these tiny dinosaurs,
prehistoric, crenellated, cast
between the tractor ruts in mud.

On the green, a junior Douglas Fairbanks,
swinging on the chestnut's unlit chandelier,
defies the corporation spears—
a single rank around the bole,
rusty with blood.
Green, tacky phalluses curve up, romance.
A gust—the old flag blazes on its pole.

In the village bakery
the pasty babies pass
from milky slump to crusty cadaver,
from crib to coffin—without palaver.
All's over in a flash,
too silently . . .

Tonight the arum lilies fold
back napkins monogrammed in gold,
crisp and laundered fresh.
Those crustaceous gladioli, on the sly,
reveal the crimson flower-flesh
inside their emerald armour plate.
The uncooked herrings blink a tearful eye.
The candles palpitate.
The Oistrakhs bow and scrape
in evening dress, on Emi-tape.

Outside the trees are bending over backwards
to please the wind : the shining sword
grass flattens on its belly.
The white-thorn's frillies offer no resistance.
In the fridge, a heart-shaped jelly
strives to keep a sense of balance.

I slice up the onions. You sew up a dress.
This is the quiet echo—flesh—
white muscle on white muscle,
intimately folded skin,
finished with a satin rustle.
One button only to undo, sewn up with shabby thread.
It is the onion, memory,
that makes me cry.

Because there's everything and nothing to be said,
the clock with hands held up before its face,
stammers softly on, trying to complete a phrase—
while we, together and apart,
repeat unfinished gestures got by heart.

And afterwards, I blunder with the washing on the line—
headless torsos, faceless lovers, friends of mine.

A Cemetery in Co Durham

The stones line up in corrugated rows
like a game of *Dover Patrol*
and the ground is full of pencil boxes.

But YOUNG CHILDREN ARE NOT ALLOWED
WITHOUT SUPERVISION because
this is where the adults play.
They to and fro to a chirping tap
and fill the rusty watering can.
The urns are pretend poppy pods . . .

Untidy as a nursery floor, with toys
and little furniture, it is a good place
to come and talk like a child to yourself—
no one is listening.

Ivy clambers over the sides of a rusty cot.
There are snails and scabs of lichen—
things to pick at while you read.
& CHILDREN-IN-ARMS ARE NOT ADMITTED
TO FUNERALS

unless a father pays the bill
for a satin box of buried treasure—
the feel of a fontanelle, buttocks
tender as a soft-boiled egg, and all
the inventory of little flesh.

Each gothic window is like an ironing board.
Mothers touch the pointed stones
as if they were irons.
They never lose their heat—
always burny, always burny . . .

Reading Her Old Letter about a Wedding

On the envelope, a frowning postmark
cancelling the familiar face.
Inside, only a day when I wasn't there :

a love-bite on the bride's young neck
not quite hidden by her creamy collar,
'like the mark left by a violin'.

Bridesmaids, three to one mirror,
opening hairgrips with their teeth.
The bridegroom's spiky tuft of hair,

the best man crossing out his opening gambit
('My Lewds, Labia and Genitalmen'),
the father tying his shoes with a double-knot,

then our horns and lavatories, lavatories,
and the old mother left behind, it says,
'like Feers in *The Cherry Orchard*'.

This is the past : that tiny synagogue,
the trodden glass, photographers,
the college lawn in regency stripes,

a boy who oompah-ed to himself
tromboning with a paper-clip,
a puppy's penis like a radish,

and you, for the first time suddenly tired . . .
the girl in a corner, forgetting everything
except your face in the mirror—

pale as the grass under a stone.
At the cemetery, I noticed how each rose
grew on a shark-infested stem.

Invalid, Convalescing

Before, the medicines glowed
like vodka, gin, madeira, whisky,
just drinks to clear the throat.

You spread yourself in bed,
a living, sprawling anecdote,
your timing always wicked, always deft.

I can still see
the oriental backscratch wielded
like a goad

when you acted Herr Professor Wittgenstein
acting ill, three days before he died—
his muted, unemphatic *nein*

before he left
the charismatic answer to some starry-eyed
tremendous half-hour question.

Today, you grimace down your booze.
You shuffle round the room
in stocking feet,

fretting for a favourite pair of shoes
which turn up in the window seat.
They've sprouted shoe-trees in the gloom.

Now, at every evening meal, a guest.
He is elegantly dressed
by Biba, Blades and Savile Row—

and asks you if you follow
as he winds and turns, precisely blurred,
elaborate, meticulous, six fittings for each word.

You blow on your broth.
Your face is mesmerized, old, tense,
white as the eight o'clock pill.

He stops. You eye the pepper mill,
pause and pick the tablecloth.
Perhaps it is a question asking for an answer . . .

Epithalamion

The orange excavator's iron arm,
limp as a lobster's claw,
points to where a thousand parsley parasols
stroll in the meadow's calm.

This grass is vintage grass—
champagne frogspit sparkles in the sun.
A tipsy butterfly lolls
and totters through the afternoon.

The river's set with silver, laid with glass.
With open, stopped and double diapason,
the weir's pipes burlesque a score—
a march arranged from Mendelssohn.

We've come too soon
against a wedding day that was not long . . .
The chestnut's trousseau broods above,
the daisies change into confetti,

and trying to make love
we only make adultery.
Here we have and hold our muddled hearts.
There, across the field, the excavator starts.

The Kipling that Nobody Read

'the Kipling who limped out of the wreckage, shrunken and wry
though he looks, has in a sense had his development as an artist'
                    —Edmund Wilson : *The Wound & the Bow*

I

All the way through Kipling's Kent
the train played snakes and ladders,
and missed a go at Eastbourne . . .

The sun stood still. Clouds moved.
Grey invalids arranged their shawls,
stonily, against the shade.

The sun stood still. Clouds moved.
A nudist colony of angels exercised
their wings in Eastbourne cemetery.

II

We saw him in the Toy Museum, Rottingdean,
a fairy contemplating other fairies—
behind glass, a dusty ballerina

pirouetted like a screw and stopped.
The last word in lace and satin
withers like a bunch of flowers.

Hair is changed to brittle sisal,
clinkered gold. His clothes
are limp as Liberace's wrist.

36

III

But at *La Belle Hélène* he takes his seat
as neatly as a folding opera glass.
His head is perfect, tanned

the shade of aspic, kept beautiful
by concentration. He wipes away
his horn-rims like a conjuror,

and doesn't smile like other people –
his teeth pose in the nude
and photograph themselves.

IV

One day he'll overwind the sun's gold watch,
and face the night, the back clicked off—
darkness, diamonds, a sense of hurry stopped.

Gethsemane

For two hours in this August twilight
the dimwit daytime owl, city-suited,
Clark Kent in harmless horn-rims,
traditionally wide-eyed,
has hooted
bits of Tate and Brady hymns.
Another has replied
with selections from Arthur Sullivan.
Now both prepare to murder through the night.

We're sleeping rough.
Our rusted ninth-grade
Morris van
looks wrecked,
abandoned, old enough
to be a place where hens have laid
and shat and pecked . . .

A cigarette ages in my hand.
The lilac smoulders into ash—
each bloom a Pisan wonder of the world,
leaning just before the crash . . .

Everything seems planned,
arranged somehow, a work of art.
We watch the foxgloves' flapping fingerstalls,
the twisting bloodied tentacles—
the moon was mother-of-pearled
until they squirted clouds of ink . . .

A church bell gives out a clink
of pencils—the distant echo of my booming heart—
and night flings back
its doors of black
like a museum devoted to rare sadnesses . . .

Dreams. Caresses.
I cannot love. I cannot sleep.
I feel the scything headlights sweep
towards this orchard sanctuary.
They rake the place, then swerve away.
We sweat and toss,
turn each new posture to a station of the cross,
and pray for day
to come to this Gethsemane.

Morning comes, frail with mist.
I unclench my fist,
to help you with your bra—each breast
a tender blister needing to be dressed.

On the Perpetuum Mobile

We met in a museum once.
The cloakroom claimed our tragic rainwear
as it dripped on parquet marked with muddy tracks—
two mackintoshes in distress
and footprints going nowhere . . .

The first editions turned their backs
or sighed discreetly to themselves
when touched and taken from the shelves.
The large four poster like a barge of state
sailed empty into emptiness three centuries too late.

We met in a museum once,
in its hush of hushed-up scandal,
and whispered platitudes in code
(while Boucher's nymph arranged her sandal)
about the innocence of naked spode.

One of Etty's nudes was hanging like a clue,
the flesh tints pinkly obvious, the shadows crudely blue.
We met in a museum once,
among the Constables and Turners,

and listened to the noise of rubber soles
that whimpered at the corners,
eking out our awkward roles
with prompts from labels on the stands.
We met in a museum—
a place for shaking, shaking,
not for holding hands.

I'd practised my straightforward laugh,
my bright attentive smile, as if God were taking
photograph on photograph.
It wouldn't do, I thought, to agonize or weep,
or be embarrassing or cheap.
I wore my expression like a promise.

We looked at Rembrandt's raddled Venus
worshipping her broken-nosed Adonis
and mocked her dimpled thighs between us,
before we reached da Vinci's failed machine
for realising what he'd never seen—
the concept of forever, eternal love,
infinity and paradise, what is beyond and what above . . .
A dusty wheel stopped by friction,
a wooden after-life, a botched-up fiction.

How well, I said, these things succeed,
how cleverly they speak of endings ending,
how effectively they plead
for nothing.

In the cafeteria
we watched how drops on marble tabletops
are joined to trembling drops
by nervous fingers, how an upset teaspoon will
cry out with brief hysteria . . .

We met in a museum once, for many years,
walked round and left by different ways.
Entering the final phase,
I noticed with a shock
the year was old
and light got bruised by 4 o'clock.

A Cremation

The Garden of Remembrance lies
like *Schlaraffenland*,
its flowerbeds pressed neatly out
with pastry forms. Beyond
those liquorice gates, the gardener—
a cook, methodically stirring
his ginger-bread mix with strange spoons, or
rolling out the marzipan.
How finely sieved the snow is on the ground,
how neatly docked and docketed the rosebush
pretzels with the price of someone's names . . .

I'd forgotten this poetic diction,
this building at the edge of town,
its elaborate architectural periphrasis
to avoid calling a spade
a spade . . .
The stock doves chortle.

Above the kitchen chimney stack,
the sky quavers on a high inaudible note.

Inside, we're at the opera,
an audience all backs and best hats—
before us a stage littered with bouquets.
We stand up like enthusiasts
and bring our hands together for
the performance of a lifetime, but
not even silence can coax the principals back.
They are shy in their wings . . .

Caruso, Gigli, Battistini, listening
to our disastrous memories of their greatness—
the vicar's untrained *sprechgesang*,
as he licks a finger to turn the page;
our own stuttering that ends on an echo;
while all the time the euphemistic curtains
close on painful silence.

Outside, above the chimney stack,
a top C moves the air to tears,
endlessly holding the note—
and the Garden of Remembrance lies
with magic dates, with magic dates . . .

PRE-RAPHAELITE PAINTINGS

The Horse

As he picks his way towards the fence,
his foreskin sways like a drop of flesh . . .

Each step has a slight caesura,
the hind legs move in slow march time.

I study the brush strokes on his hide,
the rind of each hoof, the polished dung.

His puffy mouth is like a boxing glove,
wet leather clenched on the snaffle :

the iron crunches as he takes the apple . . .
and the long head is almost a skull,

with sudden khaki teeth
and crater nostrils—

almost Holbein's blur across the canvas.
Flies are feeding near the eyes.

Old Woman at the Breakfast Table

Dim gold-glow in the chrysalis
around a hinge of spectacle.

Crushed coriander's heavy odour
from black bread on the table.

On her neck there are crumbs of flesh,
small, shadowcasting crumbs.

White curtains are breathing in and out,
and the poems of Pushkin read themselves.

She bends to blushing diagrams
in a catalogue of corsetry.

With her lips ajar,
she attends to sunsets in her lap.

Along the edge of a window-frame,
dugs of paint are warmed with sun.

She is wrinkled like a very new flower,
with pelican's pouch,

slide of bicep-breast,
and the elbow nipple's untidy complication.

From golden onion towers of teeth,
her tongue pronounces only pinkness

to the sun and air
which is the son and heir.

Chestnut Trees

Suddenly there are little green vultures
hatched from varnished petits fours.

They perch like envious angels, plotting
in groups of two and three, with cloak wings.

I was expecting a more expansive gesture,
a coup d'état, not these little stings of green

that will go through a pineapple stage . . .
Things seem, well, frivolous—

the wych elm buds and wafts its drying
fingernails, careful to keep them apart.

In the autumn martyrdoms,
tonsured heads will fall.

Return Ticket

'& yet I would fain be at the Beginning of my Willows growing.
Nite sollahs, and rove pdfr. Farewell Md Md FW FW FW Me Me
lele lele—and lele aden'

—Swift : *Journal to Stella*

The train, of course, is running away.
Listen, listen—it learns a new language,
chanting strange words again and again.

Left behind, the traffic lights
exchange three words across the street,
blinkered in Jane Austen bonnets,
like the three sisters longing for Moscow.
But the signpost heron stretches wings
to Didcot only, and Wantage,
and Henley. The usual
tractor plays the same gramophone record
it's always played . . .

And the crow calls *Howzat*
above a drowsy team of sheep
who go on fielding, fielding, fielding.
All the pylons go for their guns
and go for their guns, endlessly—
no wonder the fields bristle
like bad-tempered dogs
and the cockerel yawns
so elaborately . . .

Nothing disturbs the placid
mobile of seagulls above a rubbish tip,
and no one does the washing-up of Maidenhead.

The city glitters like a forme of type,
Paddington shines like a skating rink,
so why not skip the page of small ads
in a country cemetery?

What is it, then, that brings us back
to stupid afternoons and stupid evenings
spent watching the Chaplin fly
who twinkles up a window-pane?

We never close
the branch-line of the heart,
its sad little, slow little sewing machine.
Listen. Listen to its richar gangridge
and close your eyes on passing lights,
their long aposiopesis . . .

Professor Klaeber's Nasty Dream

High September hedges,
and the sun's great golden vowel
beating gold on turquoise paper.

Wild with wild dog-rose,
the hedges' medieval manuscript,
magnificent with flies.

Hazel scrolls of dusty vellum,
soft asterisks of pollen,
and the brambles wound in endless dipthong—

September's undecipherable,
September's unreadable beauty,
beyond all letters—

for the ampersand uncurls its sleepy green.
M's fly away, slowly beating over barley.
At the pond, all the Q's have changed to frogs.

Wind brings a dandelion drift of exclamation marks,
and the thrush types an @ against a stone.
Umlauts fall and splash.

But there is no way into the house,
except by the typewriter's sinking steps.
Reapers come with question marks . . .

The pince-nez falls and swings—
a dead percentage sign,
bumping like a heart against the heart.

Nature Study
(for Rona, Jeremy, Sam & Grace)

All the lizards are asleep—
perched pagodas with tiny triangular tiles,
each milky lid a steamed-up window.
Inside, the heart repeats itself like a sleepy gong,
summoning nothing to nothing.

In winter time, the zoo reverts to metaphor,
God's poetry of boredom :
the cobra knits her Fair-Isle skin,
rattlers titter over the same joke.
All of them endlessly finish spaghetti.
The python runs down like a spring,
and time stops on some ancient Sabbath :

Pythagorean bees are shut inside the hive,
which hymns and hums like Sunday chapel—
drowsy thoughts in a wrinkled brain.

The fire's gone out—
crocodiles lie like wet beams,
cross-hatched by flames that no one can remember.
Grasshoppers shiver, chafe their limbs
and try to keep warm,
crouching on their marks perpetually.
The African cricket is trussed like a cold chicken :
the sneeze of movement returns it to the same position,
in the same body. There is no change.

The rumple-headed lion has nowhere to go
and snoozes in his grimy combinations.
A chaise longue with missing castors,
the walrus is stuck forever on his rock.
Sleepily, the seals play crib,
scoring on their upper lips.
The chimps kill fleas and time,
sewing nothing to nothing.

Five o'clock—perhaps.
Vultures in their shabby Sunday suits
fidget with broken umbrellas,
while the ape beats his breast
and yodels out repentance.
Their feet are an awful dream of bunions—

but the buffalo's brazil nut bugle-horns
can never sound reveille.

Sports Day in the Park

The marquee huffs and heaves a sigh
like Gulliver's grimy white shirt,

impatient with the ropes and pegs,
and then the wind drops, but not before

the children in the hundred yards
have blown and fluttered like petals

down the grass to the flickering tape.
Ungainly grace—soufflé-ed plimsolls,

the camembert plush of childrens' vests,
the purity of ironed shorts . . .

For a moment, truancy from time,
and an OAP carefully rolling his own :

two trembling hands raise the tissue
to his trembling tongue—

poor flautist of the husky notes.
His patchy mongrel pants like an iris

where shamrock fans forget
to blur. Hot breath of August.

The trees are done to crackling.
A helicopter comes and canes the sky.

Tonight the giant is locked in—
on the gate, a padlock swings,

swings and sucks its baby toes . . .

Home for the Elderly

Whale-bone and iron. It is
a seaside town inland. Waves comb in
over the beach's bald spots.

Ladies are anchored to handbags.
Shells in the ear tell of tides
and a wheezing wind.

Blood pressure and lumbago
have left these shrimps—
pink and puffed as a rowing eight, slumped
over their needles.

Outside, a dog chases its tail
like a miniature railway . . .

Lobsters struggle in their walking frames,
wear warm mittens all year round.
Sprouting eyebrows twitch like rods
at the end of a pier.

The Crab is arthritis playing scales
and other pleasures—
a Cornish pasty crimped and kept for weeks,
a concert party with a chorus line of legs,
the idea of Australia, hairy
with the names of coastal resorts
where nephews live . . .

Thumbs twiddle like wind gauges.
They feel the hurricane that does not blow
from north or south or east or west,
and hold the furniture in heavy seas—
while I stand like a chestnut tree
looking for an ashtray.

Danse Macabre

Two queers heel and toe it down the High,
and fling their arms about like tic-tac men.

Magdalen Tower secures its health
with a massive course of acupuncture.

In his summer shirt, a bobby's notebook
bulges squarely like a nursing breast.

Hearing a cry, he begins to un-
button with finger and thumb.

A man has collapsed on the pavement.
We frown at the blue of this early Picasso

who nervously pats his hair, and tries
to straighten the watch on his wrist.

The crowd gathers like pain—
sailors crouching for a hornpipe . . .

Kublaikansky

He recollects the grain on milking hands, *kumiss*,
the shiver in the mare's suede muzzle;

hailstones in a gleaming terra cotta dish
like mothballs, *klukva*, or the roes of fish,

when thunder eased itself to drizzle.
Or swans in summer, drifting treble clefs,

the *nyanya's* nipples, lavender on blonde dumb breasts,
a brother sucking like a metronome.

The dew-drop on a bullock's pizzle,
thick glycerine, a limpid gum,

swaying on the great dead thistle.
Trunks of fir-trees, each a St Sebastian's martyrdom;

the beetle moving slowly in its trireme;
the beach's button box; the simpleton

whose finger wrote his speech in air; sweet-corn,
onyx gooseberries, *kasha* and the curlew's scream.

Frost or sunshine wrapped the pools in cellophane;
leaves blinked in the rain;

and night and day were dazzle-bright
with asterisks of bird-shit ...

His overcoat is black with hieroglyphics,
a garbled alphabet of twigs and hay.

59

He puts his lips to the lip of the glass
so tenderly that the people who pass

throw handfuls of copecks
to drive him away.

Ember-eyed, he starts his bitter music—
sentimental chords sucked from a sour honeycomb.

RHYMING CUFFLINKS

The Behaviour of Dogs

Their feet are four-leafed clovers
that leave a jigsaw in the dust.

They grin like Yale keys and tease
us with joke-shop Niagara tongues.

A whippet jack-knifes across the grass
to where the afghan's palomino fringe

is part Opera House curtain, part
Wild Bill Hicock. Its head

precedes the rest, balanced like
a tray, aloft and to the left.

The labrador cranks a village pump,
the boxer shimmies her rump,

docked to a door knocker, and
the alsation rattles a sabre—

only the ones with crewcuts fight.
Sportif, they scratch their itches

like one-legged cyclists sprinting
for home, pee like hurdlers,

shit like weightlifters, and relax
by giving each other piggy backs . . .

All Together for the Dawn Chorus

The doves work out like quarterbacks,
touching between their toes.

They are Othello's men whose heads
do grow beneath their shoulders.

They hold their breath like duvets,
because they are thinking of bed . . .

And the bluetit in his uniform
of powder paints and spectacles—

he nods his crew-cut head in time
and eats a breakfast worm like

someone tugging off a pair of tights
While the pigeons coo and woo, I stroke

the scratchiness of your sow's ear
and wait the miracle of silk.

Defective Story
(for Laurien Wade)

A line of teal puts fifteen stitches in the sky
and the evening is losing blood.
Too late, the rain types out the tragedy—
the City's gone to St John's Wood.

The Lunatic, a cunning Cantonese,
avoids pursuit in Regent's Park,
where all the autumn trees
are Chinese waiters in the dark.

So many bowls of birds' nest soup,
held aloft on branching fans
of fingertips, were bound to dupe
the night sky and its radar scans.

Meanwhile, the bristling bloodhounds of the sea
lift the flesh along their backs,
foam at the mouth dramatically,
and drop their heads to sniff for tracks.

To take the culprit by surprise,
the sea scrawls W's with childish hand,
and—the master of disguise—
cultivates its farming land.

The waves are miles wide of the mark :
they sweep up tidily to pass the time
till Sunny Jim—a brighter spark—
investigates the crime.

A clock explodes, but no one wins :
the mind picks up its old conventions.
The game is up and life begins
with only three dimensions.

Beware the Vibes of Marx

At the thought of personal extinction,
pulmonic and aortic veins become emphatic,
the respiration quickens, is erratic—
signs (like Köchel numbers) of intellectual distinction.

His resonant, suggestible pineal gland
enjoys the witty vibes of Marx,
the mythic bass of Roland Barthes
and other members of the bland.

His mind is alienated, solipsist :
the mammiferous and sexually seductive,
if real at all, can only be reductive.
He'd rather finger Bach than Liszt.

Though sleep is existentially synonymous with death,
his orthodoxly Freudian Id is powerless to stifle
an after-life primordial, Jungian and archetypal—
materialist in Paradise, he dreams of earth :

the sharp umbrella's umbra fades,
the soft penumbras of the parasol
have lost their definition. Illogical
but positive, he ponders meaning and its shades.

The Ayer grows problematic, dark.
Which premise logically entails
the fifteenth day of March and sails—
a street of blue-black sails like shark.

Insurance, Real Estate, &
Powders Pharmaceutical

In the panelled, sound-proofed Penthouse Suite,
the Big Cheese contemplates the creases in his pants,
practises putts and (depressive) swallows down his stimulants.

Outside his doubledoors, a sunray (dusty) from the street
projects a movie on the parquet floor. Willie the Seam
(10 stitches) (with a hernia from humping the adding machine)
gingerly crosses his legs in the beam—
a double-cross performed on screen.

Hank (with hepatitis) checks his eyeballs (topaz) in a spoon,
eases down a (saffron) inch of milky cuff,
and dreams (*Take a TRAIN—Vacation SOON*!)

(O that lush Miami scene!) Life is tough
at Insurance, Real Estate & Powders Pharmaceutical
(Protection, Pitch & Dope): whole days are spent
easing back a cuticle,
buffing shoes, receiving rent.

One night, round six or so,
(quite likely) wearing shades, a janitor
from Lethe Co.
(the wrong side of the tracks)
will slam (impossible) the sliding door
and make them die of income tax.

Two Circuses Equal One Cricket Match

'But their lowd'st Cannon were their Lungs;
And sharpest Weapons were their Tongues'
—Marvell : *Upon Appleton House*

A Roman circus. Gladiators, strong men come,
awkward in armour, from their pavilion.
Mail-fisted thugs who drub
the helpless air with clubs . . .
A flying gore of red, red admirals
turns our picnic to a bacchanal :
we eat our goodies
on grass strewn pink with prostrate bodies.

Imperious, you mount a nag of thirty hands
and trample me into the ground.
Whoosh ! your lips expectorate a stream
of self-igniting gasoline.
The gullet, tongue and vocal chords
accommodate a host of swallowed swords . . .
I emulate the stoic Greek
and Seneca, until the pollen shrieks
inside my streaming, red-raw abattoirs . . .
The membranes detonate like joke cigars.

Trees creak and yawn, boo in the wind.
Two spotless spinsters, penned
behind wire-mesh, *Meltonian*-white
with vestal fright,
lollop like performing elephants.
Red-nosed clowns in classic baggy pants
stagger round in braces, martyrs to the heat . . .
The autumn audience hurls its rotten fruit.

ANNO DOMINI

and then Leander I make a
dyer's son, about Puddle-wharf . . .
　　　　　　—Bartholomew Fair

I   The Corporation Gardener's Prologue

Is moder add im layde in live—
a nonely child an cymbal—
Þe fader too add striggen years,
an for a bid was speegeless.

Deedoadal John on Sadderdaies, on margged daies,
in cass-doff ladies' camel coad, in sangwedge board—
an aygell wooded-wigged—falsetter voyse, cryigg :
rebend, rebend, for evans add and.

Þe orwriggle bud addernoydle,
is ayre sligged doun wid rain,
adbonnyshig þe basser-bye.
On weegdaies wergyng in þe parg :

clibbig grass an straydenyg þe paths,
dedousyg werbs for vibers.
E warders þe loobyns, e warders garnations :
red-ott pogers, hollyhogs babbtized bye and.

Þe warderyg-can cries
on þe bingushions of moss.
E breeches undo abble trees,
bud will not warder a solidree rose—

Undill id droobs and wildes
an wildes an droobs
aboud ids thursday wilderness.
Þe pedals dribbig doun þe thorns.

70

II   *Verdi's Requiem*

Names, any names, the purest names,
the ordinary names of the lost—

John K Wakefield, Will Kennair, the sanitation engineer.
Sedgewick & Parkin, Solicitors—

lost golden names, painted on the Flemish large,
sun-gilt on the sea of frosted glass :

(& Commissioners for Oaths).
Charlie Hutchinson, the barber.

Rufus Peddlety and Cecil Atwood,
later Matthew 'Matty' Lancaster,

official of the Inland Revenue.
A dozen names—

once repeated slowly by the Registrar
and written down in steady copperplate.

His cufflink catches the light :
letters wrestle in gold.

The Registrar writes
Thomas Eric Corner and underlines the last

as if it were important.
Twelve ordinary names

chiselled on stone.
Atwood, Anson, Tillotson, Calvert—

names of the bones.
Gravel forces off their finger nails,

and the cabbage whites with caviar eyes
stare about this stony paradise.

Recordare, Jesu pie,
quod sum causa tuae viae :

ne me perdas illa die.

III   Birth

In Tommy Morton's byre—
but the child, when it came, was perfect.

Milking the Friesian,
squeezing the softness, pinging the pail—

soft chandelier of stalactites :
the shifting legs prop up the hundredweights of dark.

And the waters broke in a little beck :
it helter-skelters slowly,

round and down my only pair of tights,
gets inside my overshoes.

The wet stone flags and the hiss of the Tilley
breathing in, and always breathing in.

The swallows came and went like carpenters,
their beaks full of twigs. A trickling tap.

But the child, when it came, was perfect.
The funny fossil of the anus,

cloacal curl coiled up in bloodied alabaster,
and the after-birth dyeing the milk in the pail.

Centuries later the light brought two of the shepherds,
the tall one picking his nose, and Douthwaite smirking.

They ran for a doctor, fetched Joe from the pub,
smelling of drink and brilliantine,

his old straw hat on the back of his head,
the nimbus of its fraying rim.

And Dr Anderson and Dr Smythe
and Dr Middleton, the senior partner,

all three of them came from the pub,
with penicillin, needles, gut.

IV Benny Bethsaida's Spectacles

Their case lies on the counter like a mussel,
and the light is drowned and forty fathoms dim.

They used to fold up neatly as a bat—
now, they lean like a broken bike

against his face, and cycle him into the sea :
spanish inks the bottom of its jar,

pear drops form a polyp reef,
and children come with starfish hands

whenever he hears the seasick bell . . .
Benny Bethsaida's famous filthy spectacles !

when I snatch them off, he rubs
the omega imprinted on his nose,

and sees a shaken brolly fill the door
with palm trees scattering sunlight . . .

I give them back cleaned up with spit.
His anxious fingers fit the frames

and nervously steer the wobbling steels
around his ears . . .

As good as new.
Lot better now. A1, in fact.

V   The Man with Hutchinson's Career

Lunchtime on a day in June and hardly a wind :
sparrows hopping—cripples all, with unseen crutches.

Lunchtime and hardly a wind.
I make them play in uniform :

jerseys grey and blazers brown,
and brown school caps with peaks.

The referee blowing his bubbly whistle.
Four of them parody the fire brigade,

pecking and pulling a piece of bread.
The seagull perches on the roof, dithers

and glides to the safety-sheet.
The starlings stride in oilskins . . .

Rufus stands with the sun in his eyes,
squinting up at the block and tackle,

suspended *Slumberland* too big for Horan's stairs.
Lunchtime, laying out the warts in rows,

and the sign—Guaranteed Cure for Warts.
And Bobby B, bad with Hutchinson's Career :

he stops to study Ernie Calvert's sheets of music,
music pegged and faded, dusty tunes.

Arms allegro, concert violinist,
invisible cymbals strapped to his knees,

persistent fingers play a virtuoso trill
and both feet work a drum.

His boots are laced up like a clarinet
with knotted string Lunchtime on a day in June,

cadenza in the rising wind :
is there anything wrong with a one-man band?

VI Square Dance at Cana

He takes the great folio Bible,
the one with studded boards and uncut pages,

undoes the clasp and rests it on his knees—
a black accordion to celebrate the Sabbath.

On the windowsill, a Waterford vase,
filled from the tap in the yard outside,

takes to itself the sunset's sweet sauterne,
and bishops move on a tipsy tangent,

a knight totters forward and then to the left
knocking over a Queen—and all things marry.

VII *Sunblest Bread & Two Tail-Ends of Cod*

His legs were short and bandy as a lyre,
a pair of empty brackets twenty inches long.

Zebbi Best, the rent man on his round,
in neat stag-beetle boots, size three,

who moved as if the soles were flapping off.
His bustle practised kerb drill like a child . . .

Poor Zebbi Best with Duck's Disease,
hidden up a sycamore, with quacking kids below,

who whispers 'Send this multitude away'
and hears a kind of answer to his prayer—

'Who wants to join my gang? Who wants
to suck a lion-tamer?' (Me, mister, me.)

But who is speaking?
Who holds the Extra-Strong Mint like a host?

Who is feeding five thousand kids
from a bottomless paper bag?

VIII   *Epileptic Fit*

A notice in the Wayside Pulpit
announces blankness to the bleaching sun,

blankness and three rusty drawing pins.
The graveyard's empty picture house

is packed with rows of shiny seats,
threadbare granite ruined with initials

and patchily plush with moss . . .
He lies, relaxed as coppernob Van Johnson

when he took the part of Rip van Winkle—
his jersey tucked into his underpants,

his features busy as the flywheel of a watch,
one eyebrow jigging like a rabbit's nose.

It is the waking which is terrible :
the stretching arms, the screaming yawn,

the way his spine curves like a ladle,
the paper face that crumples up . . .

Beside the cemetery, allotments,
and a crusted sty with rooting pigs

who rummage in the swill
like women at a jumble sale.

Floppy hats, high-heeled trotters,
massive hams, a double row of buttons

done up neatly, salmon pink on beige—
they squeal and stub their noses out,

flushed and burning with the change of life . . .

IX   *Jew The Obscure*

In Oxford, in Christ Church, in Tom Quad,
I sway, and hiccough like Greenwich Mean Time . . .

Its clapper clenched like a boxing glove
of bronze, the great bell tolls and tolls.

The college Mercury counts the shadows out,
his finger raised like a referee.

O the contest is over, is over—
he is mounting a bike to cycle home

like a dog lifting its jodhpur leg,
the perfect *attitude en arrière* . . .

But while the crickets wind their watches up,
I stagger like a miracle and walk on water . . .

X   *The Italian Doctor with the Roman Nose*

Trumpets of the Coundon Silver Band
barabb—babba—baa   barabb—babba—baa

and the doctor washing his hands,
trickling tap and Wright's Coal Tar.

Outside where Redworth Road meets St John's Place,
the drum is afraid, the drum is so afraid—

worn skin and hollow bumping carapace.
Barabb—babba—baa the bugles brayed . . .

Who will remember
that once I heard

the Requiem by Verdi
in the Free Trade Hall at Manchester,

or how I liked two sugars in my tea,
well stirred?

Who will dream my face
as white as wedding sheets, my lips

vague as laundered bloodstains?
Who will trace

in sleep the outline of my hips?
Or hear the heart in every blood-filled gland

jerking like a second-hand?
Will anything remain?

Tuba mirum spargens sonum
per sepulcra regionum

barabb—babba—baa
barabb—babba—baa . . .